Billy Graham
in the
SOVIET UNION

By Bob Terrell

Novosibirsk Orthodox Cathedral

Tallinn Oleviste Baptist Church

Novosibirsk Baptist Prayer House

Moscow, The Cathedral of the Ephipany

Bob Terrell is the author of numerous books and articles, and lives in Asheville, North Carolina. He has traveled frequently with Billy Graham in the United States and overseas, and accompanied Mr. Graham on his visit to the Soviet Union in 1984.

Photography by Russ Busby
Book Design by Barbara Pontes

Contents

4 *Moscow street near the Kremlin.*

A Personal Word
from Walter Smyth

During the 35 years I have been privileged to work with Billy Graham there have been many highlights. During those years God has opened doors for the preaching of the Gospel in many parts of the world and given us many memorable experiences. But none is more unforgettable than the trip to the Soviet Union in September, 1984.

It was unforgettable for many reasons. For one thing, for many years it was an opportunity we never expected we would have. "I didn't think it would ever be possible," Mr. Graham told his team associates later. As is well known, the Soviet system is based on an atheistic ideology, and religious belief is not encouraged. That Mr. Graham was permitted to preach—with no restrictions on his message—in churches in four major Soviet cities was truly a remarkable turn of events. And yet it happened, as you will see in the pages of this book. Over and over during our visit I was reminded of the words of the Bible: "See, I have placed before you an open door that no one can shut" (Revelation 3:8).

This visit was memorable also for the response to the Gospel we saw. In every city, and in every church, the people listened intently and a high percentage indicated their desire to follow Christ as Lord and Savior. It was especially thrilling to see large numbers of young people in the services. We came away with a deep conviction that God is at work in the lives of many people in the Soviet Union.

I will always remember as well the numerous private gatherings and discussions Mr. Graham had. Some were with church leaders, some with ordinary Soviet citizens, some with ranking leaders of the Soviet government. But in every instance—without exception—Mr. Graham took the opportunity to share his faith

(Above) Moscow, August 1978, Dr. Walter H. Smyth shaking hands with two representatives of the Baptist Church in Novosibirsk, Siberia. Dr. Alexander S. Haraszti (seated on the right).

in Jesus Christ, and his conviction that true and lasting peace can only be found in Christ. He also spoke of his hope for better relations between our two countries, and his concern about the international arms race and the threat of war. At the same time, he listened and learned about the lives and hopes of Soviet citizens, and the situation of the churches today.

The September, 1984, visit took place only after a long period of intense preparation and numerous discussions with both church and state officials. Mr. Graham's first visit to a socialist-communist country in Eastern Europe was to Hungary in 1977. That historic visit marked a milestone in Mr. Graham's ministry, and helped open the door to further visits to preach in East European countries: Poland (1978), East Germany (1982), and Czechoslovakia (1982).

In May, 1982, Billy Graham made his first official visit to the Soviet Union at the invitation of the head of the Russian Orthodox Church, Patriarch Pimen of Moscow and All Russia. Patriarch Pimen had called an international gathering of religious leaders (both Christian and non-Christian) to discuss the responsibility of religious believers for peace in the nuclear age. Mr. Graham went as a speaker and observer at the conference, and preached as well in the Orthodox Cathedral of the Epiphany and the Moscow Baptist Church. At the time, he expressed the hope he might have the opportunity to return to the Soviet Union for a more extended visit to preach in major cities outside Moscow.

A major role in preparing each of these visits was played by Mr. Graham's personal representative for Eastern Europe, Dr. Alexander S. Haraszti. A native of Hungary, Dr. Haraszti had been uniquely prepared by God for this ministry. Before leaving Hungary in 1956, he had been a pastor for twelve years in Budapest, and had served as well as a professor at the Baptist Theological Seminary in Budapest. His experience of working in a Marxist society during those years gave him unparalleled practical experience and insights which would be invaluable in preparing the way for Mr. Graham's visits in Eastern Europe. Now an outstanding surgeon in Atlanta, Georgia, in recent years Dr. Haraszti has devoted a major part of his time away from his medical practice so he could assist in the preparations for these visits. He has worked tirelessly to open the door, and has had an indispensable part in developing this new phase of Mr. Graham's ministry.

Dr. Haraszti and I first visited the Soviet Union together in 1978. Since that time Dr. Haraszti, Dr. John Akers (Special Assistant to Mr. Graham in his Montreat, North Carolina, office), and I have made numerous trips to acquaint Soviet officials with Mr. Graham's ministry and discuss plans. Some of these trips were to Washington, for discussions with officials of the Embassy of the U.S.S.R.; others were to the Soviet Union. During the five month period before Mr. Graham's 1982 Moscow visit, Dr. Haraszti visited the Soviet Union five times. A further dozen trips to the Soviet Union were necessary before the 1984 visit— the majority undertaken by Dr. Haraszti. I joined him on several of these trips. I will always be grateful for the close cooperation I have had with Dr. Akers and Dr. Haraszti; without their insights and dedication this phase of Mr. Graham's ministry would never have taken place.

A special word of gratitude must be given for all those church and state officials in the Soviet Union who cooperated to make the visit a reality. It is impossible to mention them all; many of them you will see in the pictures which are included in this book. However, we are especially grateful to Patriarch Pimen of Moscow and All Russia, and to The Rev. Andrei Klimenko and The Rev. Dr. Alexei Bichkov of the All-Union Council of Evangelical Christians-Baptists of the U.S.S.R. Their kindness in extending the invitations to Mr. Graham and his party on behalf of the Russian Orthodox Church and the All-Union Council—as well as their warm Christian fellowship—will always be remembered with gratitude. His Excellency Mr. Vladimir Kuroyedov of the Council for Religious Affairs of the U.S.S.R. also played a vital part in making the trip a reality; we also are very grateful for the detailed work and cooperation extended by Mr. Vladimir Fitsev of the Council. We are thankful also for the indispensible role of His Eminence Metropolitan Filaret of Minsk and Byelorussia, Chairman of the External Affairs Department of the Russian Orthodox Church. The vision and the patient work of Metropolitan Filaret and his staff were vital links in accomplishing the goals of the visit. We recall especially the splendid organizational work done by Father Vladimir Nazorkin of the Office of the Moscow Patriarchate. Father Vladimir Sorokin and The Rev. Michael Zhidkov accompanied us on the trip as official representatives of the Russian Orthodox Church and the All-Union Council, respectively; their work and their warm spirit of Christian fellowship were a source of deep appreciation and affection on the part of all of us. The Rev. Ilia Orlov of the All-Union Council not only acted as Mr. Graham's interpreter on many occasions, but had worked intensely with us in the preparatory stages. Mr. Vasily Makhnev of the Moscow Patriarchate was Mr. Graham's very able interpreter in Orthodox Churches. To the many others who played a role in each city we visited, we express our heartfelt thanks.

My special thanks go to Bob Terrell for writing the text of this volume; Bob was with us during the visit to the Soviet Union, and his keen eye for detail and lively writing style make this not only a chronicle of the trip but a vivid picture of what we felt and learned. Barbara Pontes has done an outstanding job in preparing the layout and seeing the book through the various stages of publication. Russ Busby has not only provided the photographs but ably assisted Barbara in preparing the book for publication. Dr. John Akers and Dr. Alexander Haraszti have given editorial direction to the project. To these and many others who helped in the preparation of this book, we extend our sincere thanks. May this book not only give you an overview of Mr. Graham's ministry in the Soviet Union, but cause you to pray for God's work in that part of the world and for those who are seeking to live for Christ in the Soviet Union. May it also challenge you to live faithfully for Christ in your daily life, and make you a more effective witness for Him.

Walter H. Smyth

Walter H. Smyth
International Vice President
Billy Graham Evangelistic Association

(Above) Moscow, May 1982 (left to right) Dr. Alexander S. Haraszti, Dr. John N. Akers and Dr. Walter H. Smyth preparing the 1984 visit of Billy Graham to the Soviet Union.

Why Billy Graham went to the Soviet Union

Nowhere in Mark 16:15 —"Go ye into all the world, and preach the gospel to every creature"—nor in any similar Scripture did Christ command His disciples to go only into the western or capitalist world. Nowhere did he say to exclude the communist world.

Thus did Billy Graham receive his marching orders from his Commander-in-Chief—and thus did he obey them.

From September 9, 1984, to September 21 Mr. Graham and a team of ten aides visited four cities in the Soviet Union in which Mr. Graham preached the Word of God.

To lay the groundwork for this trip—and to preach the Gospel of Jesus Christ—Mr. Graham had made four previous preaching trips into the communist countries of Eastern Europe. He preached first in Hungary in 1977, next in Poland in 1978, finally in East Germany and Czechoslovakia in 1982. He also made a five-day trip to Moscow in 1982 to be an observer and deliver a major address on the subject of "The Bible and World Peace" to an international conference of religious leaders. During that visit he also preached in a Russian Orthodox Cathedral and The Baptist Church in Moscow. Finally in 1984 the doors of the Soviet Union swung open to Mr. Graham and his team for a more extended preaching mission. It was the fulfillment of a dream Mr. Graham had had for many years.

Prayer, Mr. Graham feels, was a contributing factor to the invitation he received from the Russian Orthodox Church, and the All-Union Council of Evangelical Christians-Baptists, to preach in the Soviet Union. "We sat in Lenin Stadium in Moscow in 1959, Grady Wilson and I," Mr. Graham said, "and prayed that some day God would allow us to preach the Gospel in the Soviet Union. We were

there as tourists, and Grady and I prayed aloud that God would open these doors." In addition, Mr. Graham knew that Christians in the Soviet Union had been praying for years for him to come.

"The churches wanted us to come," Mr. Graham said, "and that was a factor. Also, the many trips that Dr. Walter Smyth (International Vice-President of the Billy Graham Evangelistic Association), Dr. Alexander Haraszti of Atlanta (Liaison Representative for Eastern Europe) and Dr. John Akers of our Montreat office made into the Soviet Union and to the Washington Embassy of the U.S.S.R. to explain who I am and what my position is on many issues—those trips contributed. The Soviets also knew that there had been some criticism of me when I went to Moscow to address their conference in 1982. But that first visit gave them an opportunity to get acquainted with me—and also gave me valuable first-hand experience of the Soviet Union."

Whatever the reasons for the issuance of the Soviet invitation, Mr. Graham and his team made a whirlwind tour of the Soviet Union from the Baltic Sea to the heart of Siberia. The evangelist preached in Russian Orthodox and Baptist churches in four major Soviet cities—Moscow, Leningrad, Tallinn, and Novosibirsk—the same Gospel that has been his worldwide message the last four decades. He also conferred with church leaders and state officials, and conversed with civic leaders and organizations in all four cities.

Wherever Mr. Graham went in the Soviet Union, he was received with warmth and graciousness by all he met.

"I came to learn about Soviet life," Mr. Graham said—and learn he did. He learned quickly that in Russian "red" can mean beauti-

ful; the birch, which is so prevalent, is the Soviet national tree; that Russian shish kebab is excellent but pickled garlic is a bit much for western tastes; that mushrooms and french fried onions are a dinner delicacy; that in Estonia people relish caviar with Pepsi Cola; and that Soviets mix Pepsi and mineral water to make a fizzy drink.

He learned that in the Soviet Union there are tourists shops where Soviet rubles are not accepted and purchases must be made in American dollars or other western currency, and that many shopkeepers use abacuses to figure change in the ancient way, and work them faster than adding machines.

Among Mr. Graham's stated goals were these:

He wanted—first and foremost—to preach the Gospel to as many people as possible. He wanted to get first-hand experience about life in the Soviet Union. He wanted to help promote good relations between the churches and the state, between the Russian Orthodox Church and other Soviet churches, and between the United States and the Soviet Union. He wanted to do what he could to promote international peace. He also wanted to stand up openly for the ultimate elimination of all weapons of mass destruction.

Mr. Graham was told that of the approximate 274 million Soviet people, only 17½ million were members of the Communist Party, while more than 100 million were religious believers of some type.

Misconceptions of Americans concerning Soviet religious life had been emphasized in the furor that surrounded Mr. Graham's 1982 trip to Moscow. He stated then that he "found a measure of religious freedom in the Soviet Union," and the statement was misquoted and twisted drastically by the world press—one of the few times, Mr. Graham said, that he had ever been so severely misquoted.

According to reliable estimates the Soviet people number about 50 million Orthodox believers, 50 million Muslims, 6 million Roman Catholics, 3½ million Jews, 1 to 2 million Lutherans, and at least a half-million Evangelical Christians-Baptists (who also include Pentecostals and Mennonites) and other Protestant denominations like Methodists, Presbyterians, Adventists, etc.

Many churches in the Soviet Union have been turned into museums, but many others are functioning churches, and believers can be seen worshipping daily in many churches. The skylines of many Soviet cities are dotted with church spires.

In the years, however, since Lenin's revolution changed the face of Russia in 1917 Christians in the Soviet Union have been forced to live checkered lives.

When Lenin came to power, he wanted to reduce the power of the state church (the Russian Orthodox Church), which had often been called the "Church of the Czars." By an edict in 1918, Lenin sharply separated the churches from the state. The Orthodox church was divested of its extensive land holdings and all schools were placed under the state. He also favored at first the smaller evangelical churches, which had been oppressed by the large state church that represented the official religion of the Czarist regime. As a direct result of this change great revivals swept Russia in the early 1920s.

When Stalin succeeded Lenin after Lenin's death in 1924, he thought the churches were a threat to his government, so he ordered the churches closed and purged the ranks of Christians. Thousands of clergy and Christian people were killed, countless others hounded and persecuted.

During World War II—known in the Soviet Union as "The Great Patriotic War"—when Stalin's back was pinned to the wall, he saw that the churches sent out pastoral letters encouraging their members to give fierce resistance to the invading Nazi armies. Recognizing the important service of the churches to the war effort, he allowed the re-establishment of the office of the Orthodox Patriarch and the founding of the All-Union Council of Evangelical Christians-Baptists. The churches continued their support of the war effort. The severe persecution of the churches and individual believers stopped during the war, and a measure of religious freedom was restored for years to come. However, religious life was still kept strictly in the background. With Stalin's death in 1953, the churches opened up even a bit more, but when Nikita Khrushchev came to power in 1958 the churches were severely oppressed again. Leonid Brezhnev's ascension to the head of the Communist Party and the Soviet government brought an ease in tension between church and state, and since that time Soviet churches have operated openly and with a certain amount of appeal.

Though Mr. Graham makes a point of saying that he believes—because he has been reliably told—that there is a certain amount of oppression, and in some areas of the Soviet Union suppression of religious freedom, nevertheless officially recognized Soviet churches enjoy religious liberties today on a scale which they have not known for decades. Some people thought that Mr. Graham was naive about the true situation of the churches in the Soviet Union. Such however was not the case. He had been thoroughly briefed on practically everything he was to encounter. He also had a deliberate strategy in order to reach his goals of preaching the Gospel, making a contribution to better understanding between the United States and the Soviet Union, and in encouraging the churches.

Lenin's Constitution of 1922 recognized the right of citizens to do both religious and anti-religious propaganda. This meant that believers could hold open air public meetings. Stalin's 1936 Constitution took away the right of believers to hold meetings outside church premises, while allowing atheists to do propaganda without restrictions. The revised Constitution of 1977 altered this slightly; non-believers may still do "atheistic" propaganda but not "anti-religious" propaganda. Believers still cannot preach outside church premises or do active and open witnessing.

Some Orthodox Churches conduct services as much as 14 hours a day, seven days a week, from 7 a.m. to 9 p.m., repeating the Divine Liturgy, a three-hour service, over and over. The Protestant churches hold two or three 2-hour services on Sunday and two or three others during the week, in addition to prayer meetings, choir practices, orchestra rehearsals, and some other specialized services. Churches are well attended.

In some areas of the Soviet Union, depending on the strictness of local committees of the Council for Religious Affairs, the children of professing Christians may not be able to gain admission to the university, and there is sometimes a tendency to give Christians the most menial jobs in some factories. But in other areas, where Christians have been recognized for their faithfulness and devotion to their jobs, Christians are often given preference in the factories because they show up faithfully for work and are reliable and hard workers.

Bibles in limited numbers are available in the Soviet Union. The government allows the printing of several thousand Bibles each year in the Soviet languages, and up to 50,000 Bibles have been legally imported in some years.

Bibles were in evidence in all the services where Mr. Graham preached, especially in the Baptist churches.

(Top center) Billy Graham addressing the International Conference of Religious Workers for Saving the Sacred Gift of Life from Nuclear Catastrophe, Moscow, May, 1982. (Top left) Patriarch Pimen of Moscow and All Russia (seated left) listens as Billy Graham preaches in Moscow's Patriarchal Cathedral of the Epiphany, 1982. (Lower) Several thousand people filled the Patriarchal Cathedral to hear Mr. Graham's message.

The Preliminary Visit
Moscow, 1982

Although he had visited the Soviet Union as a tourist in 1959, it was not until 1982 that Billy Graham made his first official visit to speak and preach in Moscow.

The invitation for the 1982 visit was extended by the head of the Russian Orthodox Church, Patriarch Pimen of Moscow and All Russia. Concerned about the ethical and moral issues facing a nuclear age, Patriarch Pimen had called an international conference of religious workers—known as the "International Conference of Re-

ligious Workers for Saving the Sacred Gift of Life from Nuclear Catastrophe"—to discuss the issue of international peace. At the Patriarch's invitation, Billy Graham attended the conference as an observer and delivered a major address on the subject of the Biblical perspective on peace.

During his whirlwind visit to Moscow (May 7-13, 1982), Billy Graham not only spoke at the conference but preached in the Patriarchal Cathedral of the Epiphany (following the celebration of

the Russian Orthodox Divine Liturgy by Patriarch Pimen). He also preached in the Moscow Baptist Church; the All-Union Council of Evangelical Christians-Baptists of the U.S.S.R. had joined the invitation bringing Mr. Graham to Moscow.

In addition, every minute of his schedule was filled with activities, ranging from visiting places of historical significance to official private meetings with ranking church and state officials. As much as was possible in so brief a time, he sought

(Above) Billy Graham with Patriarch Pimen, Moscow, 1982. On the left is Metropolitan Filaret of Minsk and Byelorussia; in the foreground (in white robe) is Patriarch Justin of the Romanian Orthodox Church.

(Left) A crowd of 2500 jammed the Moscow Baptist Church to hear Billy Graham in 1982. His interpreter was the Rev. Mikhail Zhidkov, one of the pastors of the church.

(Below) The leaders of the All-Union Council of Evangelical Christians-Baptists with Mr. Graham and Dr. Walter Smyth (of the Billy Graham team) in Moscow, 1982.

to listen and to learn all he could about Soviet society, and particularly about the situation of religious believers and the churches in the Soviet Union. He also spoke on every occasion about his personal faith in Jesus Christ, and his conviction that Christ alone was the ultimate answer to the problems facing the human race.

At the conclusion of this first visit Billy Graham stated it had indeed been one of the most memorable trips of his entire ministry. At the same time, he was aware that he had seen only a glimpse of the Soviet Union and its people, and he expressed the hope that it might be possible for him to return for a more extended visit in the future to see other areas and preach in various cities besides Moscow. Although brief, the 1982 visit set the stage for the expanded preaching visit Billy Graham was able to make to four major Soviet cities in September, 1984.

NORWAY

SWEDEN

FINLAND

POLAND

Baltic Sea

TALLINN

LENINGRAD

White Sea

CZECHOSLOVAKIA

HUNGARY

MOSCOW

ROMANIA

RUSSIAN SOVIET FEDERATED SOCIALIST REPUBLIC

Black Sea

Caspian Sea

NOVOSIBIRSK

Lake Bai*

Aral
Sea

TURKEY

IRAN

IRAQ

MONGOLIA

PEOPLE'S REPUBLIC OF CHINA

AFGHANISTAN   PAKISTAN

INDIA

+ NORTH POLE

Arctic Ocean

+3 +4 +5 +6 +7 +8 +9 +10 +11 +12 +13

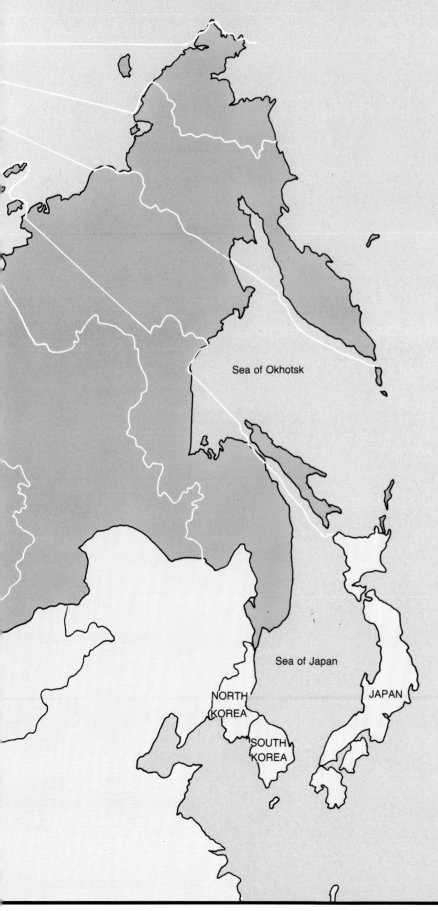

Sea of Okhotsk

Sea of Japan

NORTH
KOREA

SOUTH
KOREA

JAPAN

Mr. Graham's 1984 trip to the Soviet Union was, in his own words, "a whirlwind tour". In twelve days, he spoke more than fifty times. His schedule began early in the morning and continued far into the night.

This scene was repeated in all the cities Mr. Graham visited—Moscow, Leningrad, Tallinn, and Novosibirsk. The tour reached from the Baltic Sea through central Russia into the heart of Siberia.

And wherever it went, the Graham team was greeted by Soviet Christians with warm hearts.

The vast territory of the U.S.S.R. covers eleven time zones from east to west (shown by the white lines).

The Second Visit:
September, 1984

LENINGRAD

TALLINN

NOVOSIBIRSK

MOSCOW

Second largest city in the Soviet Union and one of the major cities of the world . . . for two centuries Leningrad was the capital of the Russian Empire . . . today it is outstanding as an industrial, cultural, and seaport city . . . founded in 1703 by Peter I the Great as St. Petersburg, the city was renamed Petrograd in 1914, and Leningrad in 1924 . . . famed as the scene of the February and October revolutions of 1917, as the besieged and courageously-defended city of World War II, and one of the architecturally splendid cities of Europe.

Located on the delta of the Neva River where it empties its waters into the Gulf of Finland, Leningrad is built upon more than one hundred islands and part of the mainland floodplain. Six hundred bridges span the six rivers that pass through the city, and those rivers, mixing with Leningrad's many waterways and canals make Leningrad the "Venice of the North." Leningrad covers 150,000 acres; its population is about 4 million.

Winters are cold. February's temperature averages 18 degrees Fahrenheit. Its snow cover lasts 132 days. The Neva freezes solid in late November and the breakup begins about mid-April.

The Russian Orthodox Theological Academy of Leningrad

Rain dripped outside the beautifully curtained windows of the Russian Orthodox Theological Academy of Leningrad. Inside, more than 600 persons, most of them students at the Academy—future priests and officials of the Russian Orthodox Church—sat spellbound in the chapel as the American evangelist talked candidly of ways to communicate the Gospel.

The room was filled with a brightness to which the students were unaccustomed. A half-dozen television cameras filmed the message, and the brilliant lights of television flooded the room.

Billy Graham's shadow played garishly on the wall behind him, fingers stabbing, hands chopping to give emphasis to his words.

Photographers moved around, tiptoeing, ducking under the beams of TV cameras—but a quietness filled the room. The students strained to hear every word. Their faces reflected their quietness, their seriousness, their eagerness, faces frozen in fascination, for this was an opportunity they were not often accorded, an opportunity to hear one of the world's great preachers tell of his own experiences in spreading the Gospel of Jesus Christ through the world.

To Mr. Graham's right, Metropolitan Antonii of Leningrad and Novgorod and Archbishop Kyril, Rector of the Academy, listened intently to the message.

"Metropolitan Antonii has written a wonderful paper," Mr. Graham said. "It is entitled, 'Christian Witness Today In A Socialist Society.' In the opening paragraphs he wrote these things: 'Our Savior said to His disciples before the ascension, "Go ye therefore, and teach all nations, baptizing them in the name of the Father, and of the Son, and of the Holy Ghost: Teaching them to observe all things whatsoever I have commanded you." Responsibility rests with the church to propagate the faith of Christ by virtue of the commandment given by our Savior to apostles and through them to their successors.'"

"With this I totally agree," Mr. Graham emphasized. "I do not go around the world preaching because I want to travel or because I like to fly in airplanes. I go because I am commanded to go and preach to as many people as I can, commanded by our Savior, Jesus Christ. I am under orders. The Commander-in-Chief has spoken, and I salute and say, 'Yes'."

Mr. Graham said the great question before the church is how to reach modern, scientific man—and from this point came the heart of his remarks.

"I know," Mr. Graham said, "that when I speak to an audience, whether it's in Africa or Latin America or Asia or Europe, or in a socialist country or a capitalist country, there are four things the audience contains:

(Below) Hundreds of students, faculty, and visitors listened intently as Mr. Graham spoke in the Leningrad Theological Academy on the theme of "Communicating the Gospel in the Modern World."

(Above) Billy Graham was welcomed to the Leningrad Theological Academy by Metropolitan Antonii of Leningrad and Novgorod (left) and Archbishop Kyril of Vyborg, Rector of the Academy. His interpreter on behalf of the Russian Orthodox Church for the entire trip was Mr. Vasily Makhnev.

"First, a sense of emptiness. Man keeps crying for something, and he never quite finds it till he finds God. He doesn't know what he's searching for. He doesn't know why this emptiness is in his heart. . . . I sense this everywhere I go.

"The second thing I notice is loneliness—existential loneliness, philosophical loneliness. Sometimes you can be in a crowd, or you may be at a social event, and for just one moment there's a sense of loneliness, even with friends. What is this loneliness? It's a loneliness for God. We were created for God, and without God there is a sense of loneliness in the universe in which we live.

"The third thing I find is guilt. All people have a sense of guilt experience. The head of a mental hospital in London said when we were there some time ago, 'If I could solve the problem of guilt, I could release half the patients.'

"And the fourth thing I notice is the fear of death. One of our greatest psychiatrists in Europe has recently said, 'The fear of death is present in our mental functioning at all times.'

"Now," Mr. Graham said, "how do we communicate with people the Gospel of our Lord Jesus Christ?

"We communicate through the cross on which He died for our sins, through the resurrection, and the Holy Spirit. How do we communicate that to modern scientific man with these four problems in his heart?

"First by authoritative proclamation. 'Faith cometh by hearing and hearing by the Word of God.' When Paul was at Corinth he said, 'For the preaching of the cross is to them that perish foolishness; but unto us which are saved it is the power of God.' If I tell the average student at a university or an average person that Christ who died two thousand years ago has been risen from the dead and is coming back to establish His kingdom some day, people laugh. It's foolish. It's silly. That's where we depend on the Holy Spirit. The Gospel has its own built-in power, no matter how it's preached."

Leningrad is a beautiful city of about four million people. The Neva River passes through the city, which stands on a number of islands. More than 600 bridges span the waterways between islands.

Upon arrival in the city, Mr. Graham and the team were taken up the Avenue of the Unconquered to visit the Piskaryovskoye Memorial Cemetery where 400,000 Leningraders who perished in the World War II 900-day siege of Leningrad are buried in common graves. The German army laid siege to Leningrad in 1941, '42, and '43, and in 1942 alone 642,000 starved to death in the city. A half-million people worked every day in the defense lines as the city courageously gave resistance to the German army's ground assaults, constant cannonading, and aerial bombardment. In the siege of Leningrad, more people died than the

(Right) At the airport in Leningrad Billy Graham and his party were met by Metropolitan Antonii of Leningrad and Novgorod.

The Piskaryovskoye Memorial Cemetery in Leningrad

(Below) The Eternal Flame at the Piskaryovskoye Memorial Cemetery recalls the indominable spirit of Leningrad—only one of four "Hero Cities"—and its citizens during the terrible days of World War Two.

(Right) Approximately one million citizens lost their lives during the 900-day siege of Leningrad. Billy Graham paid his respects to the heroism of those who fought against Hitler's invading forces by visiting the Piskaryovskoye Memorial Cemetery, where 400,000 are buried in mass graves.

(Below) At the Piskaryovskoye Memorial Cemetery Billy Graham laid a wreath in honor of those who died during the siege of Leningrad. The 900-day siege, he declared, should remind all humanity of the need to work toward world peace. The inscription on the wreath stated, "God forbid that it should happen again. Billy Graham, United States."

combined war dead of the United States and Great Britain in World War II. Two and a half million people were trapped in Leningrad, 400,000 of them Jews, and by January of 1942 more than 4,000 a day died, a high percentage of whom either starved to death or died of scurvy. Many froze to death, especially in that bitter winter of 1941-42 when the temperature plummeted to 40 degrees below zero. After the War the city was given the coveted distinction of "Hero City"—one of only four cities so honored.

At the cemetery, where funereal music played constantly, a crowd of a hundred spectators stood silently for 40 minutes, out of earshot, while Mr. Graham spoke to a small contingent who accompanied him to the cemetery for a wreath-laying ceremony. They stood hushed, looking silently toward Mr. Graham, unable to hear him. Afterward he went over to shake hands and greet those who had waited.

Mr. Graham also spoke with representatives of various governmental and civic organizations (including the Council for Religious Affairs, the Leningrad Peace Committee, leading scientists, and church leaders) many of whom went through the siege.

(Above and right) The Russians are famous for their hospitality to foreign guests. At the Leningrad Theological Academy Mr. Graham and his team were graciously given a luncheon by Metropolitan Antonii.

(Left) The librarian of the Leningrad Theological Academy showed Mr. Graham through the library, which includes many foreign theological volumes.

Mr. Graham told the audience to proclaim the Gospel with authority, with simplicity, and with urgency.

"Not only do we communicate by proclamation," Mr. Graham said, "but also by living a holy life. The Apostle Paul said, 'I keep my body under discipline.'

"We communicate the Gospel by our love. 'By this shall all men know that you are my disciples, if ye have love one to another.'"

He told the students also that we communicate the Gospel by "our compassionate social concern, by forgiving each other, and by our excitement about Christ.

"In some societies," he concluded, "you cannot go outside and preach as in others. Every society is different. How do you proclaim the Gospel? Take the fifth chapter of Galatians. We bear the fruit of the Spirit, such as love, joy, peace, longsuffering, gentleness and kindness, and self-control. People will see you, and after a while they will say, 'What makes you different?'

"You may go through hard circumstances and you may suffer, or maybe you will go to prison like the Apostle Paul and Silas in Philippi. What were they doing, moaning and crying? No! They were singing—and even the jailer came to Christ!

"So we are to bear the fruit of the Spirit, and people see the way we live and they're drawn to the Christ who lives in us."

Mr. Graham's message to the Academy was videotaped, and Father Vladimir Sorokin, a professor at the Academy, said it would henceforth be used in the Homiletics Department to teach young priests how to preach and how to spread the Gospel.

"This," said one professor without reservation, "could change the style of preaching in the Orthodox Church."

Dr. Walter H. Smyth, Vice-President of International Ministries for the Billy Graham Evangelistic Association, also thought Mr. Graham's talk to the students might have far-reaching effects.

"To me," Dr. Smyth said, "the most important address of this trip may have been the one at the Academy. That one address reached the future clergy and could have a lasting effect on the Orthodox Church."

Since Leningrad was the first city in which Mr. Graham preached, services in which he participated there set the tone for those on the remainder of the trip.

(Above) Metropolitan Antonii of Leningrad and Novgorod exchanged gifts with Mr. Graham in the Metropolitan's office.

(Below) Metropolitan Antonii (on Billy Graham's left) and Archbishop Kyrill (on his right) share some informal moments of conversation at the Metropolitan's residence.

The Holy Trinity Cathedral of the Alexandr Nevsky Lavra

In sharp contrast to the preaching appearance Mr. Graham made in 1982 in the Russian Orthdox Church of the Epiphany in Moscow (in which he had to preach with no amplification, using an interpreter who did not speak loudly enough for the large crowd to hear him), when he went into the huge Holy Trinity Cathedral of the Alexandr Nevsky Lavra in Leningrad to deliver his first 1984 sermon in an Orthodox church, conditions were right.

The crowd of 6,000 was the largest to which he would preach on this trip, and the amplification system was excellent. Every word he said went into eager ears in every nook and cranny of the great cathedral.

(Right) Billy Graham preaching in the Holy Trinity Cathedral of the Alexandr Nevsky Lavra in Leningrad. Metropolitan Antonii of Leningrad and Novgorod is seated on the right.

(Below) At least six thousand people filled the Russian Orthodox Holy Trinity Cathedral to hear Mr. Graham's sermon.

The service that day was unprecedented in the Orthodox Church. The three-hour Divine Liturgy, which began at 9 a.m., was halted at 11 a.m. by Metropolitan Antonii who extended warm greetings to the American evangelist and his team. The Metropolitan introduced Mr. Graham to the throng as "a great preacher and a great peacemaker," then invited him to speak.

Mr. Graham preached on "The Glory of the Cross," and in his sermon he said, "Crucifixion was the most terrible death a person could die. They put nails in the hands, a crown of thorns on the brow, a spike through the feet, and they hung the victim on a cross. Jesus was on the middle cross; on each side was a thief hanging on a cross. They were guilty—but Jesus was guilty of no sin. One of those thieves turned to Him on the cross and said, 'Lord, remember me when thou comest into thy kingdom.' That is the greatest illustration of faith in all the New Testament. 'Remember me! Re-

(Above and below) Billy Graham was introduced to the congregation by Metropolitan Antonii, and then preached on "The Glory of the Cross".

member me! Remember me!' And I can assure you today that God remembers you. He knows all about you and He loves you."

Later in the sermon, he emphasized that point again. "If you forget everything else that is said here today," he said, "I hope you will remember that God loves you."

Dr. Smyth was impressed with that meeting, too. "It was a complete and total breakthrough," he said. "That a Baptist preacher could come in and address an Orthodox crowd like that—in the middle of the Divine Liturgy—is totally unprecedented."

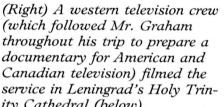

(Right) A western television crew (which followed Mr. Graham throughout his trip to prepare a documentary for American and Canadian television) filmed the service in Leningrad's Holy Trinity Cathedral (below).

(Above) Leningrad's newly-renovated Baptist Church is noted for its 100-member choir.

The Leningrad Baptist Church

The most emotional service on Mr. Graham's tour was the one in the Baptist Church of Leningrad. Three thousand persons attended that evening, jamming the inside of the church, filling every seat and every aisle, with about 500 others standing on the outside listening to the service over loudspeakers.

The pastor, the Rev. Peter B. Konovalchik, was an emotional man, easily moved to tears by the momentous occasion. As he prayed, members of the congregation prayed, their lips moving to form the words of their own prayers. Their extreme reverence was as touching as the picture of their faces—young faces, old faces, weathered, worn, warm, and tear-streaked, far from the stoic faces that most Americans connect with Russian people. The kerchiefed heads of the women splashed the church with color, and as Mr. Graham began to preach on the Twenty-third Psalm, the crowd pressed closer, standing tightly packed, shoulder to shoulder, front to back. All eyes were riveted on the podium, and here and there hands holding microphones emerged from shoulder height, the better to record the message on tape recorders.

The message Mr. Graham brought was the same Gospel that he preaches all over the world: "Jesus Christ is not dead on the cross. He is a living Christ and tonight He is willing to come into your heart, into your family, into your great country, and change your hearts. He is alive!" And the people devoured every word.

Mr. Konovalchik explained that the Leningrad Baptist Church has 3,000 members. It holds services on Sunday at 10 a.m., 2 p.m., and 6 p.m., and during the week on Tuesday and Thursday evenings, and Saturday afternoon. It has Bible studies on Monday, and choir practice for its three choirs on other days. Each service lasts at least two hours.

"Young people study the Bible during choir practice," Mr. Konovalchik said. "Some young people preach. We have twenty-seven lay preachers in our church.

"There are seven other Baptist congregations in and around Leningrad that we help," he said. "We volunteer our young people to preach and sing. We send money and Bibles."

There are two official Pentecostal groups and some small independent Baptist groups in Leningrad also.

(Above) Billy Graham being greeted by believers at the front of the Leningrad Baptist Church. The inscription above the door says "Prayer House of Evangelical Christian Baptists."

(Below) The overflow congregation in the Leningrad Baptist Church— over 3,000 people—filled every aisle and balcony as Billy Graham preached.

(Left) Mr. Graham's interpreter in the Leningrad Baptist Church was the Rev. Sergey Nikolaev. The pastor, the Rev. Peter Konovalchik, is in the foreground.

(Below) The crowd in the Leningrad Baptist Church included people of all ages, who listened reverently to Mr. Graham's message. Many responded to the invitation to commit their lives to Jesus Christ.

(Above) Leningrad's Hermitage Museum contains one of the finest collections of fine art in the world, including many famous religious paintings. (The above by Peter Paul Rubens.)

(Above) At Leningrad's Jewish Synagogue Mr. Graham had discussions with leaders of the Leningrad Jewish community.

(Below) Before the service Pastor Peter Konovalchik and various church leaders received Mr. Graham in his study. On the right is the retired pastor of the church, the Rev. Sergey Fadukhin.

(Above) In Leningrad Billy Graham met with representatives of various civic organizations under the auspices of the Leningrad Peace Committee. As he did on similar occasions in other cities, Mr. Graham shared his conviction that Jesus Christ alone could bring lasting peace: peace with God, peace in the human heart, and peace between men and nations.

The Leningrad War Memorial

On the way to the airport for the flight to Tallinn, the capital city of Estonia, Mr. Graham visited the Leningrad War Memorial, which pays tribute to all those who died and those who defended Leningrad during the siege. This spectacular memorial also displays historical artifacts of the siege of Leningrad.

"I think it is very moving that you remember the dead," Mr. Graham said. "This is one of the most moving memorials I have ever seen."

(Above and left) Leningrad War Memorial of the 900 day siege.

Tallinn Estonia

Capital and cultural center of the Baltic State of Estonia, now the Estonian Soviet Socialist Republic. (Although the government of the United States has never officially recognized the incorporation of the Baltic states of Latvia, Lithuania, and Estonia into the Soviet Union, since it took place in 1940, before the signing of the peace treaties ending World War II). . . . population 450,000, located on Tallinn Bay of the Gulf of Finland, 90 kilometers across the gulf from Helsinki . . . Fortified settlements existed here from the late first millennium BC . . . 1154 is the date of first documentary reference for Tallinn . . . Captured by the Danes in 1219, who built a fortress on Toompea Hill . . . trade flourished . . . In 1346 the Teutonic Knights bought the city . . . Peter the Great captured it in 1710 . . . remained a Russian city until it became capital of independent Estonia from 1918 to 1940 . . . occupied by Germany 1941-1944 and severely damaged . . .

Many relics of Tallinn's long history survive or have been restored, especially on Toompea Hill and in the old, walled Lower Town. Tourists from around the world marvel at Tallinn's links with the distant past.

(Above) In Tallinn, the capital of Estonia, Billy Graham met with Vice President Madam Meta Vannas and other members of the Presidium of the Supreme Soviet of Estonia. Metropolitan Alexei of Tallinn and Estonia and the Rev. Robert Vosu, Baptist Superintendent of Estonia (left) were among the church leaders who participated in the meeting.

In Tallinn, a storybook town beside the Baltic Sea, capital city of the tiny Soviet State of Estonia (population 1.5 million) Billy Graham met with the Vice-President of the Presidium of the Supreme Soviet of Estonia, Madam Meta Vannas, and other members of the Presidium, as well as church leaders and officials of the Council for Religious Affairs.

At the Presidium in Estonia, around a huge conference table, seated in heavily padded chairs with intricately inlaid wood designs, Mr. Graham shared with the Vice-President his fears of nuclear warfare, his hopes for worldwide disarmament, and his belief that the answer to these problems lies within the pages of the Bible.

"Nothing is more important," said Madam Vannas, "than to know each other and understand each other."

"I believe the Bible is the sacred Word of God," Mr. Graham told her, "and I base my beliefs on what the Bible says. I appreciate the fact that I have been invited here by the churches to preach the Gospel of Christ, which I believe has the basic answer to peace.

"I agree that the peace now is a very fragile thing and we're living in perhaps the most dangerous time in history.

"I am not for unilateral disarmament. I don't believe Americans should lay down their arms unless we have an agreement.

"In Moscow at the 1982 International Conference of Religious Leaders I called for the eventual elimination of all weapons of mass destruction. But where do these weapons come from? They didn't create themselves. They are not going to explode themselves.

"That's where I believe the Bible has an important place in society. The churches I have found in the Soviet Union are for peace, and all the polls taken indicate that a majority of American people want peace.

"But the question is how to attain peace? Human nature has not changed in all these centuries. There is still jealousy and hate and murder and from time to time terrible things happen in our countries—and these things come from the human heart. This is why Jesus Christ died on the cross. From the Christian point of view, He died to save us from our sins and to bring peace and joy and fulfillment and happiness to our lives.

"Jesus is called the Prince of Peace and when He comes into our hearts He produces peace.

"I have been told there are about fifteen nations now with the nuclear bomb. I am not concerned that the Americans or Soviets will drop the first bomb. We're too wise and too afraid for that. But with the proliferation of these weapons, some little nation may explode a bomb that will set off a chain reaction. War could even start by computer accident. That's why we must come to the conference table and go straight for the elimination of all weapons of mass destruction. If we take years going for SALT Two, Three, Four, Five, and so on, it will be too late. We must go immediately to eliminate them.

"And so I would like to see the leaders of the nations of the world that possess these weapons—and they must be led by the Soviet Union and the United States—come to the table and say we're going to eliminate them.

"I come back to the original words I made that the Bible has the final outline for peace: love in our hearts for each other, love for our enemies, and forgiveness."

At this point one of the participants asked Mr. Graham, "Do you love Communists also?" Without hesitation he replied, "Yes, every one of them. And Jesus Christ also loves them."

This was basically the same message Mr. Graham carried to the various civic committees and leaders with whom he met, and he wove this message into the Gospel he preached in various churches.

(Below) At a special luncheon in Tallinn's Hotel Viru Billy Graham greets Estonian church leaders and thanks them for their invitation to visit Estonia.

From the carved stone pulpit of Tallinn's historic medieval Oleviste Baptist Church (above left), Billy Graham preached to an overflow crowd in this large church (above right). His interpreter into Estonian was the Rev. Yuri Puusaag; in a small side chapel 400 people also heard Mr. Graham's sermon translated into Russian.

The Oleviste Baptist Church

Mr. Graham stayed two days in Tallinn, preaching in the Oleviste Baptist Church, the largest Baptist Church in the Soviet Union, and in the famous, beautiful Orthodox Cathedral of Alexandr Nevsky, named for a national hero of Russia and a saint in the Russian Orthodox Church. He also addressed a gathering of 350 Baltic area ministers in Tallinn's Rock Baptist Church.

In the Oleviste Baptist Church, speaking before the largest Baptist crowd he would face in the Soviet Union—4,500 people—Mr. Graham and his son, Franklin, observed a milestone in their ministries.

"Tonight," Mr. Graham told the audience through his interpreter, the Rev. Yuri Puusaag, "is an historic moment for me, because it's the first time that my son and I have participated together in a service."

(Above) Church leaders from all over the Baltic states of Lithuania, Latvia, and Estonia gathered in the Oleviste Baptist Church for the service. Third from left is the Oleviste Church's pastor, the Rev. Ulo Meriloo.

Franklin had given greetings, read Scripture for his father, and said an opening prayer.

"I was at my son's ordination," Mr. Graham said proudly, "when he was ordained to the ministry, but this is the first time we have participated in a regular service together."

He stood on historic ground when he made that statement, for the church in which he preached dated to the 13th Century. It was constructed in the early 1200s as a Roman Catholic Cathedral, later became a Reformation Lutheran Church in this predominantly Lutheran country, and in 1950 the building was obtained by the Baptists.

The church is located in the quaint "Lower Town" or "Old Town" of Tallinn, a section of the city that dates to medieval times, and to reach the church, Mr. Graham and his team passed over ancient, narrow cobblestoned streets lined with people. Police held the overflow from the packed church behind barricades a block from the church.

Two choirs sang from the high lofts in the rear of the church, with full orchestral accompaniment. They sang Baptist favorites, including "Do Not Pass Me By" and "When The Roll Is Called Up Yonder." An interpreter said these were songs Russian Baptists also sang a hundred years ago when the denomination was started in the Czarist Russian Empire.

From Toompea Hill, which overlooks both the "Lower Town" and the modern Baltic seaport city of Tallinn (population 450,000) one can see the spires of the city's twenty-two churches. They dominate the skyline. The most prominent building is the Oleviste Baptist Church with its towering steeple.

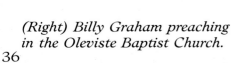

(Right) Billy Graham preaching in the Oleviste Baptist Church.

The Orthodox Cathedral of Alexandr Nevsky

(Above) Tallinn's Russian Orthodox Cathedral of Alexandr Nevsky, where Mr. Graham preached.

(Right) Against the backdrop of the elaborate icon screen in the Cathedral of Alexandr Nevsky in Tallinn, Billy Graham preached to the congregation following the celebration of the Russian Orthodox Divine Liturgy. At center is Metropolitan Alexei of Tallinn and Estonia.

Mr. Graham spoke to hundreds of people in the Orthodox Cathedral of Alexandr Nevsky, a beautiful building with onion-topped towers.

Metropolitan Alexei greeted Mr. Graham as "the profound peacemaker," and called the meeting "a wonderful opportunity to pray for peace together, and together fight hand in hand for the preservation of peace on our planet."

"We all want peace," Mr. Graham replied in his message, "and we work for it and pray for it, but too often we leave out one important thing: the Prince of Peace.

He preached on Moses and the burning bush, telling how Moses became leader of the Israelites when they most needed a strong leader. "The world today is searching for a leader," he said, "and that leader is Jesus Christ. Jesus said there is only one door, and He is the door."

As Mr. Graham preached in the Cathedral of Alexandr Nevsky (above), young and old alike listened intently to his message

(Above) Overview of Tallinn's Russian Orthodox Cathedral of Alexandr Nevsky during Mr. Graham's sermon.

(Left) Archpriest Valdimir Sorokin, Dean of St. Nicholas Cathedral in Leningrad and Professor of New Testament at the Leningrad Theological Academy, traveled with the Graham team throughout the trip representing the Russian Orthodox Church. Here at Tallinn's Cathedral of Alexandr Nevsky, Father Sorokin points out details of the Orthodox Divine Liturgy Service to Mr. Graham.

The Rock Baptist Church

(Above) These children welcomed Mr. Graham and his team with flowers.

Pastors and other church leaders from throughout the Baltic States filled Tallinn's Rock Baptist Church to hear Billy Graham speak. The Estonian people are noted for their love of music; the Baptist Youth Choir, which participated in the special service, impressed the team with their appearance and music. Mr. Graham's son, the Rev. Franklin Graham (above left), also addressed the gathering.

(Above)Billy Graham arriving at the Rock Baptist Church in Tallinn to address the meeting of ministers and church leaders.

(Left) Outside the Rock Baptist Church Mr. Graham greeted church members.

The Kirov Fishing Farm

Among Mr. Graham's favorite memories of the Soviet Union, he said, is that of "a little girl eating soup." He was on a visit to the gigantic Kirov Collective Fish Farm, which stretches along most of the coastline of Estonia and has headquarters in Tallinn, when he espied the little blonde-haired girl. She was a kindergarten student who sat primly with others having lunch when Mr. Graham passed through the kindergarten. The evangelist knelt beside the little girl, who gave him a broad smile while she continued to eat her soup. He spoke a few words to her and commented on how cute she was.

The kindergarten children, whose parents worked at the collective fish farm, were polite, well-dressed, handsome children who could have been mistaken by sight for kindergarten students anywhere in America except for the names on their lockers: Marco, Pirez, Mai, Vieko, Prut, Mariko, Mari, Angeli, Rauno. . . .

They were Estonian, a proud people who still speak their own language. When Mr. Graham addressed the crowds in Tallinn's churches, his words were translated into Estonian and then into Russian for the Russian-speaking people who attended.

(Above) Outside Tallinn Mr. Graham and his party toured the social facilities of the Kirov Fish Farm, a large collective fishery which stretches along the Estonian coast.

(Below) At the Kirov Fish Farm Billy Graham greeted youngsters at the collective farm's kindergarden. They were having lunch when he arrived.

43

(Above) Franklin Graham, on be-half of his father, visited the headquarters of the Lutheran Church in Estonia, where he was received by Probst Eerik Hisjaru. Probst Hisjaru represented Arch-bishop Edward Hark, the head of the Estonian Lutheran Church, who was out of the country. The Lutheran Church is the largest denomination in Estonia.

(Right) Franklin Graham repre-sented his father on a number of occasions. Here he greets Eston-ian church leaders at a luncheon in Tallinn.

(Above) Billy Graham presented copies of one of his books to Estonian church leaders during a luncheon.

(Left) Mr. Graham's visit attracted the attention of the press in every city he visited. Here he is interviewed by a correspondent in Tallinn.
Veteran Washington Journalist Ed Plowman (third from the right) accompanied Mr. Graham throughout the trip as press liaison.

45

(Above) Street scene in Tallinn, a bustling seaport city and industrial center. Tallinn is also a magnet for tourists, who delight in the narrow cobblestone streets and stone buildings of the "Lower Town", some dating back to the Middle Ages (right).

Novosibirsk
Siberia

A young city on the Western Siberian plain . . . Novosibirsk is the heart of Siberia . . . located four time zones east of Moscow, or 3,300 kilometers . . . by Aeroflot it is a four-hour flight from Moscow to Novosibirsk; by Trans-Siberian Railroad, stretching 10,000 kilometers across the USSR, which spans eleven time zones, it is a 52-hour train ride. . . .

Situated on the Ob River where the Trans-Siberian Railroad crosses the river, Novosibirsk was founded as a city in 1893, and has grown spectacularly this century to 1,400,000 inhabitants. . . .

Though isolated on the Siberian plain, Novosibirsk is not an unknown city. Its academic and scientific community has aroused international interest . . . The economy of the region is largely agricultural. . . . Novosibirsk is the major shipping point for the vast mineral wealth of the area.

A hundred years ago this was a village, a brief stopping point on the Trans-Siberian Railroad; now it is a sprawling industrial city, already the third largest city in area and the eighth largest in population in the Soviet Union.

Products made in Novosibirsk are exported to many countries.

ПОЛЕЗНЫЕ ИСКОПАЕМЫЕ СИБИРИ И ДАЛЬНЕГО ВОСТОКА

(Above) Siberia is a vast storehouse of natural resources, many of which have yet to be utilized. At the Museum of Geology at the Academic City outside Novosibirsk, Mr. Graham and his party were briefed on Siberia's mineral wealth.

The Academic City

At the turn of the 20th Century, Novosibirsk was a small village, a brief stopping point on the Trans-Siberian Railroad, which spanned this vast territory. Now, Novosibirsk is a sprawling city of 1.4 million people, the capital of Western Siberia, and the eighth largest Soviet city in population and third largest in area, behind Moscow and Leningrad. Novosibirsk is situated 3,300 kilometers—four hours by air or fifty-two hours by rail—east of Moscow, almost directly north of Delhi, India.

Siberia is huge, and partly because of that, it has also been one of the world's most mysterious places. That veil of mystery has begun to rise as Siberia emerges to take its place among the world's most blessed areas in resources. In area, Siberia is 18 percent larger than the United States. It contains more than half the territory of the Soviet Union, but only about nine percent of the Soviet population. Its people number only 24 or 25 million, and to attain that figure it had to double in the last twenty years.

Siberia is an area of vast agriculture, industry, and science. Descending by airplane to the Novosibirsk airport, we saw huge areas under cultivation that could best be sized by square miles rather than acres.

Billy Graham compared Siberia with the American West during the West's development period: a vast expanse of seemingly unending natural resources—oil and gas, gold, timber, waterpower. Siberia contains more than half the world's coal, and its oil and gas fields are massive.

Siberia's development has been more rapid than that of the American West, and will probably continue to be because it can employ the modern tools of technology to move through its infancy. Already its products are exported to many countries. From an economic point of view, Siberia would seem to be the Soviet Union's future.

Mr. Graham and his team saw evidence of the wealth of Siberia at the Academic City, outside Novosibirsk. There, they toured the Museum of Geology and saw thousands of samples of gems and minerals mined in Siberia. Then the group visited with academic and research leaders of the Institute of History, Philology, and Philosophy of the Siberian Division of the USSR Academy of Sciences.

The director, Dr. Anatoly P. Derevyanko, a professed atheist, gave the Graham party a brief, interesting peep into history.

"We theorize," Dr. Derevyanko said, "that man came first to Siberia 300,000 to 400,000 years ago. Here we try to correlate Siberian Man with the peoples of China, Manchuria, and other areas—and, of course, America.

"The United States and the Soviets," he said, "are solving an important problem together—that of who was the first man in America.

"It was not Columbus," he laughed. "We have discovered that 25,000 to 30,000 years ago, the first man to stand in the New World was a man from Siberia.

"At that time," he joked again, "we had closer relations than now. A great land bridge connected our continents and man passed over the bridge from Siberia to America. Then the Bering Channel began to exist and separated the continents.

"We in the Soviet Union and anthropologists from the United States are working closely together on this part of history."

"I am very interested in this," Mr. Graham replied. "I took my college degree in anthropology. The best professor I had was a Russian. My professors held the view that the first Americans came from Siberia, and I have always held that view myself."

"The first Siberians and Americans were Animists," Dr. Derevyanko said. "They believed in nature and that nature was alive. They believed a bear was a man in other clothing, that he had a soul like a man. They believed this of other animals, also.

"Every ancient tribe in the world," Dr. Derevyanko said, "had a religion of its own—or an idea of the world. Marx and Lenin dealt with knowledge of the world." Then he asked Mr. Graham, "Have you read Lenin and Marx?" "Yes, I

(Above) At the Academic City the Director of the Institute of History, Philology, and Philosophy of the Academy of Sciences of the U.S.S.R., Academician Anatoly Derevyanko had a lively discussion with Mr. Graham about a number of topics, including religion.

have," the evangelist replied. "Have you read the Bible?" The scientist admitted he had. Then Billy Graham turned to Dr. Haraszti and said, "Alex, do we have any more Russian Bibles?" The answer was affirmative, and he presented four Bibles to the group as well as copies of his most recent book, *Approaching Hoofbeats*, which includes the text of his 1982 Moscow address.

It was not only "ancient tribes" in Siberia that had religions of their own—many present-day Siberians profess religious belief, too.

(Below) Billy Graham visited the Academic City, a large world-renowned research and educational complex outside Novosibirsk, and was briefed on its work.

(Right) At the Novosibirsk airport Mr. Graham was met by church officials, including Archbishop Gedeon of Novosibirsk and Barnaul (on Mr. Graham's left) and Archpriest Dimitri, Dean of the Russian Orthodox Cathedral in Novosibirsk (far left).

(Above) People in the Soviet Union love flowers, and presented them to Mr. Graham and his team on many occasions. Novosibirsk was no exception, and the team felt the warmth of those who greeted them in spite of language barriers.

(Right) Upon arrival in Novosibirsk, Mr. Graham responded to the official greeting to Archbishop Gedeon of Novosibirsk and Barnaul, (left) and Baptist Superintendent Konstantin Borodinov (second from right).

50

(Left) In Novosibirsk Billy Graham had a fascinating discussion with one of the Soviet Union's leading cardiologists, Professor Eugenij Meshalkin (left), and several of his associates.

(Above) Before the service in the Novosibirsk Baptist Church Billy Graham met with Siberian church leaders. He was briefed on the work of the Baptist churches of Siberia by the Rev. Konstantin Borodinov, Baptist Superintendent of Western Siberia (standing, left) and the Rev. Yakov Fast, pastor of the Novosibirsk Baptist Church (standing next to Mr. Borodinov).

(Above) The choir of the Novosibirsk Baptist Church joins the congregation in singing a hymn. The inscription behind the choir reads "We Preach Christ Crucified." At center is the Rev. Yakov Fast, pastor of the church.

The Novosibirsk Baptist Church

The Rev. Konstantin Petrovich Borodinov, the Baptist superintendent of Western Siberia, said he works "in four large areas that contain 54 Baptist churches." One was the Baptist Church of Novosibirsk where the Rev. Yakov Fast has baptized eight hundred Christians into his congregation in the last ten years. The church stands on a bluff overlooking the winding Ina River where baptismal ceremonies are held out of doors in good weather.

In this district, the Rev. Borodinov said, there are 5,000 Baptists and many more Russian Orthodox than that. The Novosibirsk Baptist Church had, at this time, 1,038 members. The church, eighty years old, has both Russian and Ukranian members, and about two hundred Germans in its congregation. The church has three choirs: a main choir, a youth choir, and a German choir.

"We have many lay preachers in our congregation," the Rev. Fast said. "Many preachers."

Every inch of space in the Novosibirsk Baptist Church was filled with worshippers when Mr. Graham came to preach on the evening of Tuesday, September 18. They were crowded closely, front to back, shoulder to shoulder, perspiring in the hot television lights, wiping their brows—and listening intently. Outside hundreds more listened by loudspeakers in windows and in a separate building

The Main Choir sang first in Russian, and the German Choir followed. The congregation seemed to be proud of the fact that it had a choir that could sing in the German language. Many people in the area are of German background, transferred to Siberia from the Volga region during World War II.

Mr. Graham said later that he did not remember ever preaching in a church more tightly packed with people than the Novosibirsk

(Above) Many were deeply moved by Billy Graham's message in the Novosibirsk Baptist Church; they had prayed for years that he would be able to visit them.

Baptist Church on this evening.

Mr. Graham prayed for better understanding between the nations, for bridges instead of wars, and for peace in our time. He prayed especially for the upcoming meeting between President Reagan and Foreign Minister Gromyko. His sermon came from the Gospel of John, and in it he said, "I was at the Academy today and we met some scientists. I thought to myself, 'We cannot prove the existence of God in one of their laboratories. We can't even come close to it.' We cannot prove scientifically that God exists, but everybody believes there is a Supreme Being. We are born with the belief that there is something beyond this life, something in control of this vast universe.

(Below) "I don't recall ever preaching in a more tightly packed church," Mr. Graham stated after the meeting in the Novosibirsk Baptist Church. The service was especially notable for the large number of young people (above).

"We had a woman in America who was born deaf, mute, and blind," Mr. Graham said. "Her name was Helen Keller. For years, they tried to communicate with her, and when they finally managed to communicate and mentioned the name of God, she said, 'I knew Him but did not know His name.'. . .

"The Bible teaches that God created the universe," Mr. Graham preached. "All those millions and millions of stars and planets were made by God. He made this earth. He made you, and because He made you He loves you. If you were the only person in this whole world, Christ would have died for you."

Hundreds of Siberian hands were lifted up when Mr. Graham gave the invitation that night to receive Christ, and as he left the church the crowd waved handkerchiefs in farewell, an old Russian custom. The haunting strains of "Till We Meet Again" in Russian followed Mr. Graham to the limousine that took him back to the city. Henceforth, when he hears the lovely melody of that song, he will think of those Christian faithful standing on the bank of the Ina River.

(Above) Following his sermon Mr. Graham said goodbye to the crowd outside the Novosibirsk Baptist Church.

(Above right) Many who could not get inside the Novosibirsk Baptist Church still found a way to listen to Mr. Graham's sermon. Altogether approximately 2,500 attended the service, many coming from other parts of Siberia.

(Below) The Novosibirsk Baptist Church is located on the banks of the Ina River on the outskirts of Novosibirsk; in good weather the church uses the river for public baptismal services.

The congregation outside Novosibirsk's picturesque Russian Orthodox Cathedral greets Billy Graham.

The Novosibirsk Orthodox Church

Throughout his stay in the Soviet Union, Mr. Graham tied Biblical thoughts in with current events and facts of life.

He told an audience to which he preached in the Novosibirsk Orthodox Church: "Some day, if God spares us a war, I predict Siberia will be the richest area in the world. But if you gain all the riches and lose your soul, what have you accomplished?"

The service of the Divine Liturgy was impressive. Like all other Orthodox churches, the Cathedral was bedecked with icons. The trappings of the church were ornate. The partition which separates the altar where the priests take communion from the congregational area of the church, corresponds with the veil in the Old Testament temple.

The priests passed in and out of the Royal Gate, the central portal through the altar wall, singing and chanting the liturgy, all under the leadership of Archbishop Gedeon of Novosibirsk and Barnaul. The heavy scent of incense permeated the air, wafting out among the standing faithful, when the Archdeacon began to pray, and translators, putting the words into English for the Graham team, revealed the basic theology of the Orthodox Church.

"Let us pray to the Lord," the Archdeacon intoned. "Bless, Oh Lord, our church."

After a few moments, he continued: "Let us pray to our Father, for Patriarch Pimen, for Archbishop Gedeon, and for the Deacons. Let us pray to the Lord of

(Above) Archbishop Gedeon introduced Billy Graham to the congregation and listened intently as he preached. Following the sermon Archbishop Gedeon presented Mr. Graham with a traditional Russian Orthodox icon.

(Left) The deep devotion of many Russian believers is illustrated by this woman, praying in the Novosibirsk Orthodox Cathedral.

the world for our country, for all the countries, for the army, for those of us who are traveling, for those who struggle with difficulty, for those who are in prison—to lead us from all sorrows and in all of our needs.

"Lord, save us by your grace and have mercy upon us."

A large congregation filled the Novosibirsk Orthodox Cathedral as Billy Graham preached (below). Mr. Graham's sermon followed the celebration of the Divine Liturgy (left), led by Archbishop Gedeon.

(Above) At a press conference in Novosibirsk Mr. Graham was asked a wide variety of questions by representatives of the Siberian media.

The Siberian press asked for an hour with the American evangelist. A half-dozen reporters, representing eighty newspapers and magazines with a general circulation of two million, posed such politically-charged questions and topics as these:

—"Give us your views on peace."

—"How would you treat the actions of those in West Germany, who work against the deployment of missiles?"

—"What are your impressions about Siberian Baptists visiting the Orthodox Cathedral?"

—"Express yourself on the politics of President Reagan."

Archbishop Gedeon broke into the barrage of harassing questions, scolding the press. "Gentlemen! Gentlemen!" he said. "Billy Graham was invited by the Russian

The moderator of the press conference said there were certain forbidden areas for the Soviet press. "We cannot delve into war propaganda," he said, "nor into anything anti-Semitic, into racial or national hatred, into anything to harm believers' feelings, into pornography, or into hatred of Soviet authorities and power."

And later that day, at a banquet in Mr. Graham's honor given by the Orthodox church, one after the other, priests rose and made ten-minute toasts to Mr. Graham, during which they recounted the victories of the "Great Patriotic War." One priest wore eleven medals he had been presented for fighting "in the front lines from first to last." One after another, they lamented the possibility of future war. The Mennonite preacher lamented longer than anyone.

"Siberia is a challenging area," Mr. Graham told the banqueters, "with many challenges still ahead.

"I have seen your concern for peace," he added, "and felt your burden, and I will take it back with me."

Orthodox Church. Please, ask him some positive questions."

—"Do you see any results of your work?" the next reporter asked. "Do you have less crime in the States?"

—"Give us your impression of Siberian churches and how the stories of them are carried in the American press."

Billy Graham and his party were honored at an elaborate farewell dinner by Archbishop Gedeon of Novosibirsk and Barnaul, attended by numerous church and state officials from many parts of Siberia (lower left). The Archbishop presented Billy Graham with a traditional Russian fur hat from Siberia (above).

(Right) Following the farewell dinner in Novosibirsk Mr. Graham met a number of pastors and lay preachers from various areas of Siberia.

Before departing, Mr. Graham quoted the last verse of the fifteenth chapter of First Corinthians to the gathered clergy: "Therefore, my beloved brethren, be ye stedfast, unmoveable, always abounding in the work of the Lord, forasmuch as ye know that your labour is not in vain in the Lord."

For four hours that evening, Mr. Graham and his team, flying on a Soviet TU-154, roughly the equivalent of the Boeing 727, followed the sunset, a brilliant flame on the horizon ahead, back to Moscow.

(Right) Upon departure from Novosibirsk, Billy Graham and his party boarded an Aeroflot Airlines jet for Moscow. Throughout their trip in the Soviet Union they flew on Aeroflot, the official Soviet airlines.

(Below) At the Novosibirsk airport Mr. Graham shares conversation with Archbishop Gedeon (on Mr. Graham's right) and Mr. Alexander Nikolaev, of the Novosibirsk Council for Religious Affairs (left).

Moscow

Capital of the Soviet Union . . . one of the world's great cities with broad, tree-lined boulevards, magnificent architecture, and beautiful statuary . . . first mentioned in chronicles dating to 1147 AD . . . a spiritual center of the Russian Orthodox Church for 600 years . . . its best-known points are at the center of the city—the Kremlin, and Red Square.

Greater Moscow, formed in 1960, covers 339 square miles and has a population of about 11.5 million people.

Located on the Moskva River, a tributary of the Oka and thus of the Volga, Moscow was occupied by Napoleon in 1812. In 1813 a gigantic rebuilding program was begun and parts of the Kremlin and the Bolshoi Theatre were constructed. In the Bolshoi in 1922 the Union of Soviet Socialist Republics was set up.

The Kremlin's crenelated red brick walls and nineteen towers were built at the end of the 15th Century. Spasskaya Gate Tower leading to Red Square was erected in 1491, a year before Columbus visited America.

Moscow also is a city of the arts, featuring 28 major theaters, 125 cinemas and hundreds of clubs in which movies are shown. In the city are 65 museums and art galleries.

Moscow is, indeed, one of the world's beautiful cities. . . .

(Above) Billy Graham preaching in the Patriarchal Cathedral of the Epiphany, the church of Patriarch Pimen of Moscow and All Russia (seated on left).

The Cathedral of the Epiphany

Mr. Graham preached more sermons in Moscow than in any other Soviet city. He preached in two Russian Orthodox cathedrals; the Resurrection Cathedral (the church of Metropolitan Filaret of Minsk and Byelorussia) and the Cathedral of the Epiphany (the church of Patriarch Pimen of Moscow and All Russia), and twice in Moscow Baptist Church, one of these a sermon to 250 Baptist pastors from all over the Soviet Union who gathered to celebrate the 100th anniversary of the founding of the Baptist Church in Russia.

(Right) Following Mr. Graham's sermon Patriarch Pimen thanked him for his message and presented him with a traditional Russian Orthodox icon.

(Left) During Orthodox services candles are burned as a symbol of the prayers of God's people ascending to the throne of God.

(Below) 5,000 people listened to Billy Graham's sermon in the Patriarchal Cathedral. A special sound system carried his message to every corner of the huge cathedral.

(Above) Patriarch Pimen, the head of the Russian Orthodox Church, introduced Billy Graham to the congregation following the celebration of the Orthodox Divine Liturgy.

(Above and below) Young and old alike listened intently to the sermon of Billy Graham in the Patriarchal Cathedral of the Epiphany.

(Above) Billy Graham preached during the Sunday morning service of Moscow's Cathedral of the Resurrection, the church of Metropolitan Filaret of Minsk and Byelorussia (on Mr. Graham's left).

The Resurrection Cathedral

In the Resurrection Cathedral, a blind choir occupied the choir box on one side of the ornate altar, and a sighted choir sang from the box on the other side. Both choirs sang beautifully through the three-hour Divine Liturgy.

The Resurrection Church's icon wall contained twenty-three paintings and reproductions of paintings which depicted the life of Christ.

(Left) Russian Orthodox worship services are marked by magnificent choral music. This is a part of the choir that sang in the Cathedral of the Resurrection.

During that service, Metropolitan Filaret ordained a new deacon.

"It was a tremendous privilege for me to be invited to the induction of the new deacon," Mr. Graham told the Metropolitan. "I was praying that God would give him a long and wonderful ministry."

(Above) Russian Orthodox worshippers stand throughout the three-hour celebration of the Divine Liturgy.

(Left) Metropolitan Filaret of Minsk and Byelorussia distributes Holy Communion to the faithful during the service. At center is Archdeacon Vladimir Nazarkin.

(Right) Father Nazarkin invites the worshippers to join in prayer.

(Below) Hundreds filled the Cathedral of the Resurrection to hear Billy Graham's sermon.

(Above and below) Patriarch Pimen of Moscow and All Russia, the head of the Russian Orthodox Church, honored Mr. Graham and his associates at an elaborate luncheon at the end of the visit. Also attending the luncheon were a number of leading church and state officials.

(Above) Following his sermon in the Patriarchal Cathedral of the Epiphany, Mr. Graham met with Patriarch Pimen in his private chambers and presented him with a copy of his book, Approaching Hoofbeats, *which includes the text of Mr. Graham's address to the International Conference in Moscow in 1982.*

(Above) Metropolitan Filaret of Minsk and Byelorussia, Chairman of the International Relations Department of the Russian Orthodox Church, invited church leaders and the Billy Graham team to a luncheon at his official residence outside Moscow.

(Left) Metropolitan Filaret presented Mr. Graham with an elaborate hand-painted lacquered box, a traditional form of Russian folk art.

(Above) Vice-Minister Vladimir Fitsev of the Council for Religious Affairs of the Soviet government greeted Mr. Graham and his party at the Moscow airport, saying he hoped the visit would promote better understanding and peace.

(Below) At a press conference upon his arrival at the Moscow airport Billy Graham was officially welcomed by representatives of the churches which had invited him, the Russian Orthodox Church and the All-Union Council of Evangelical Christians-Baptists.

(Above) At Moscow's ultramodern airport Billy Graham was met by leading church officials and members of the media.

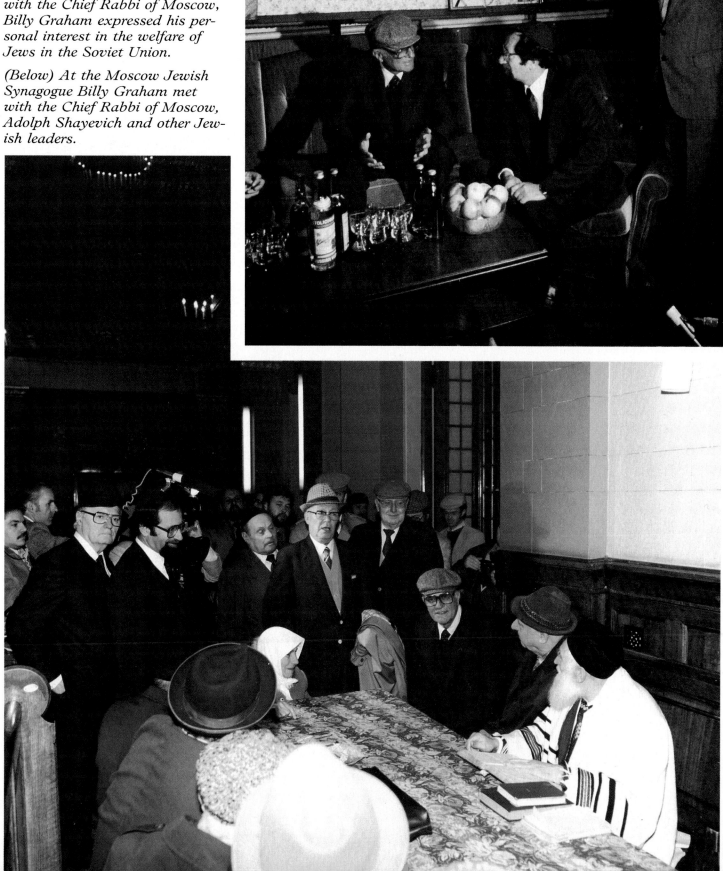

(Right) During his discussions with the Chief Rabbi of Moscow, Billy Graham expressed his personal interest in the welfare of Jews in the Soviet Union.

(Below) At the Moscow Jewish Synagogue Billy Graham met with the Chief Rabbi of Moscow, Adolph Shayevich and other Jewish leaders.

During his visit Mr. Graham was received by His Excellency Boris N. Ponomarev, a member of the Politburo and Chairman of the International Relations Department of the Central Committee of the Communist Party of the Soviet Union. Their one-hour-and-forty-minute discussion covered a wide range of issues.

(Right) Following Patriarch Pimen's luncheon in Moscow, several leading officials said farewell to Mr. Graham. To Mr. Graham's immediate left is Minister Vladimir Kuroyedov of the Council for Religious Affairs; at his far left is Dr. Georgi Arbatov, Director of the Institute of United States and Canada Studies. To his right is Vice-Minister Vladimir Fitsev of the Council for Religious Affairs.

(Below) Academician Georgi Arbatov (third from left), the Director of the world renowned Institute of United States and Canada Studies, received Mr. Graham and his associates. He was flanked by his co-workers, who are outstanding Soviet experts in their fields of research.

(Left) Metropolitan Filaret of Minsk and Byelorussia, Chairman of the International Department of the Russian Orthodox Church, gave Mr. Graham a special miniature icon as a remembrance of his visit.

(Below) Mr. Graham gave a copy of his book Approaching Hoofbeats *to Mr. Yuri Zhukov, the Chairman of the Soviet Peace Committee.*

Why did they listen so intently? Why did they soak in every word, seeming not to want to turn loose of even the smallest syllable? Professors, laborers, housewives, nurses, washerwomen, secretaries sat entranced. Some faces were grim; some smiled slightly, not in amusement but in obvious pleasure at what they heard and experienced; some were almost in tears.

Tape recorders were evident all over the church. Cassette tapes of Mr. Graham's messages would later be distributed in many parts of the Soviet Union.

Mr. Graham talked of the obstacles that block our way to peace in the world and peace within ourselves. He recounted times when people had told him they were miserable. He said Senator Ted Ken-

The Moscow Baptist Church

Moscow Baptist Church was packed for the 5 p.m. service. Every seat was filled and every inch of standing room occupied when Billy Graham stepped to the pulpit to preach on "Hope for the Future." The choir in the balcony had sung beautifully, accompanied by a full orchestra with strings. Two soloists with operatic voices thrilled those who came to hear the American evangelist.

There in a country governed by self-professed atheists, the tall American preached the Gospel to 1,200 people. He spoke in a foreign tongue, his words translated into Russian by Ilia Orlov, Vice Chairman of the International Department of the All-Union Council of Evangelical Christians-Baptists, and a preacher and organist in this very church—Moscow Baptist.

The people listened intently. Mr. Graham's voice echoed from every corner in the church building.

"I am the way, the truth, and the life," he quoted Jesus Christ. "No man cometh unto the Father, but by me."

(Right) A capacity crowd filled the Moscow Baptist Church for Mr. Graham's sermon on "Hope for the Future."

nedy had made the statement in the United States Senate that forty wars are going on in the world right now.

"Men used to fight with swords and spears," Mr. Graham said. "Then they began to fight with guns, and we had the First World War, and then the Great War in which so many of the people of this country were killed. And now we stand talking about another war.

"What is wrong?" he asked. "Man's heart is wrong. That's the reason Jesus said, "You must be born again.' You must have a change of heart. He said, "I can change your heart. I can make you a new person.'

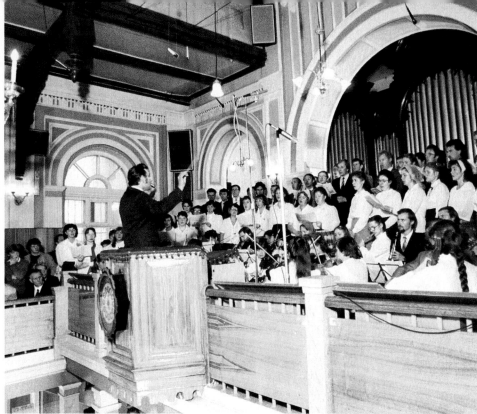

(Right)A special orchestra accompanied the choir of the Moscow Baptist Church during the service.

(Below) The Rev. Ilia Orlov interpreted for Mr. Graham at the Moscow Baptist Church. At left is the Rev. Dr. Alexei Bichkov, General Secretary of the All-Union Council of Evangelical Christians-Baptists of the U.S.S.R. At right is the Rev. Vasily Logvinenko, Senior Pastor of the Moscow Baptist Church.

"No way out? Jesus said, 'I'm the way!'"

Vasily Logvinenko, senior pastor of Moscow Baptist Church, said later to Mr. Graham: "You have sown here the seeds of peace and love."

(Below) Large numbers of young people were present wherever Mr. Graham preached in the Soviet Union.

(Above) Many responded to Mr. Graham's invitation in the Moscow Baptist Church to follow Jesus Christ as Savior and Lord.

(Left) The Rev. Andrei Klimenko, President of the All-Union Council of Evangelical Christians-Baptists of the U.S.S.R., welcomed Billy Graham to the Moscow Baptist Church.

Mr. Graham considered his talk to the Baptist pastors and area superintendents at the Jubilee Conference, commemorating one hundred years of Baptist mission work in the Soviet Union, as one of his most important talks in Soviet territory.

(Below) 1984 marked the 100th anniversary of the beginning of organized Baptist mission work in Russia. Several hundred pastors and other church leaders from all over the Soviet Union gathered in the Moscow Baptist Church to hear Billy Graham speak at a special service commemorating this event.

Jubilee Seminar of the All-Union Council of Evangelical Christians-Baptists

Mr. Graham touched on Christian life and history in the Soviet Union in this talk.

"I have found in my travels here so far that you have much to teach those of us who are Christians in other parts of the world," he said. "Your faith and your dedication to the Gospel of our Lord Jesus Christ is inspiring, and like St. Paul declared concerning the Christians in Rome, 'I thank my God through Jesus Christ for all of you because your faith is being reported around the world.' . . . Your history has

brought to my mind the periods of misunderstanding and even active persecution that you have endured and the faithfulness of thousands of believers to Jesus Christ even in the midst of these threats. . . . God has called you to be His servants within a society which has strong atheistic propaganda. You have special challenges and difficulties that would be unknown to me in my society. But I have challenges and difficulties in an affluent, materialistic, so-called free country that may be unknown to you. . . .

You are witnessing to non-believers; you are witnessing to people who do not know the Bible; you are witnessing to people who haven't had a personal experience with Christ. One mistake that is made, I think, on the part of some people in other parts of the world about America, they say, "Oh, you come from a Christian country.' No, I don't! Ours is not a Christian country. It is a secularistic, materialistic country. There are many Christians in America but they are not the dominant force. Many times people say, "How can America do this if they claim to be Christian?" But all that is done is not Christian. The Christian faith should not be judged on the basis of what America does politically or in some other way."

Mr. Graham talked to the pastors about "things that do not change in the midst of change."

He said this was a politically, socially, and scientifically-changing world, but in the midst of all these changes, he said there are things that do not change:

"The nature of God has not changed," Mr. Graham said. "In Malachi 3:6 He says, 'I am the Lord, I change not.'"

"The Word of God has not changed," Mr. Graham said, citing Isaiah 40:8, which reads, "The grass withereth, the flower fadeth: but the word of our God shall stand forever," and Psalm 119:89: 'For ever, O Lord, thy word is settled in heaven.'

"Thirdly, the moral law has not changed," Mr. Graham said. "All through the Scripture the Ten Commandments are the same. That has not changed.

"Human nature has not changed," he continued. "Jeremiah said in 17:9, 'The heart is deceitful above all things, and desperately wicked: who can know it?'

"Our social responsibilities have not changed. Love thy neighbor as thyself. There is the story of the Good Samaritan which describes who our neighbor is: a person from another part of the country, another race, another background, another ideology. Wherever there is need. We are to love them no matter who they are. We are to love the believers and the non-believers. That's what Jesus did. 'By this shall all men know that ye are my disciples, if ye have love one to another.'

"God's promise to be with us in all circumstances has not changed," Mr. Graham said. "And, lo, I am with you always, even unto the end of the world.

"Finally, God's way of salvation has not changed. In Acts 4:12 the Apostle Peter said, 'Neither is there salvation in any other: for there is none other name under heaven

(Above) The Jubilee Service commemorating the 100th Anniversary of organized Baptist mission work in Russia.

given among men, whereby we must be saved.'

"Jesus said, 'I am the way, the truth, and the life: no man cometh unto the Father but by me.' A hundred years ago there was only one way to go, one way for forgiveness of sin, and that was through Christ. The way of eternal salvation is through Christ. That is what your Baptist missionaries in Russia preached a hundred years ago. And today there is still only one way.

"But there is another way we preach: By the Holy Spirit producing the fruit of the Spirit in our lives. In some parts of the world you may not verbalize your faith, but we can love, we can have tenderness, and the Scripture says, 'Against such there is no law.' No

one can tell you that you cannot love your neighbor.

"So I leave you today with love in my heart for you, with deep appreciation for the privilege of being here. I will always remember that I had a small part in your Jubilee. I wish you God's blessings wherever you are. Be faithful to Christ in whatever situation He has placed you, and I promise God and you today that with all my strength with the years I have left, I want to be faithful where God puts me.

"People ask me, 'When are you going to retire?'" Mr. Graham concluded his remarks to the Russian preachers. "Never! Not until God retires me, and then I'll be in heaven and I'll see you there.

"God bless you!"

(Below) The Rev. Andrei Klimenko, President of the All-Union Council of Evangelical Christians-Baptists of the U.S.S.R., introduced Mr. Graham at the 100th Anniversary service.

(Right) Mr. Graham met in Moscow with leaders of independently-registered Baptist churches, which are independent of the All-Union Council of Evangelical Christians-Baptists.

(Below) The leadership of the All-Union Council of Evangelical Christians-Baptists of the U.S.S.R. gave a memorable dinner for Mr. Graham and his associates. During the dinner the Rev. Dr. Alexei Bichkov extended greetings to Mr. Graham and gave him a letter from a woman who had committed her life to Christ during his 1982 visit.

(Above) At Moscow's World Trade Center Billy Graham held a press conference at the close of his visit to the Soviet Union. A large number of reporters from both Soviet and western news agencies questioned him about his impressions of the Soviet Union, its churches and human and religious rights. In his release Mr. Graham assured reporters that he had raised the issue of human and religious rights repeatedly in his private discussion with government and church officials.

(Below) The night before leaving Moscow Billy Graham thanked those who had helped organize his visit to the Soviet Union at an informal dinner in his hotel, the Hotel Sovetskaya.

(Above) At the Tomb of the Unknown Soldier of the Soviet Union, at the foot of the Kremlin Wall, Billy Graham laid a memorial wreath and prayed for world peace.

The Message

"My primary purpose in coming to the Soviet Union was to preach the Gospel of Jesus Christ, just as I have done in many other parts of the world. There have been no restrictions on my message, which is the same message I have preached throughout my ministry."

"He died a terrible death, but He didn't stay on the cross. They buried Him, and then He was raised from the dead. He is alive! Jesus Christ is not dead on a cross, and tonight He is willing to come into your heart, into your family, into your great country, and change your heart. He is alive! Do you know Him personally?"

—Baptist Church, Leningrad

"Jesus met the world, the flesh, and the devil—and He conquered! He is the conquering Christ, and our authority over the evil in our hearts is the name of Jesus Christ. Does Jesus control your life? Does He control your heart? He can tonight. Open your heart to Christ tonight and say, 'I want to be a true follower of Christ.' "

—Oleviste Baptist Church, Tallinn

"If Jesus Christ is still dead then all our Christian faith has no meaning. His death on the cross, where He shed His blood and His body was broken, would have no meaning without the resurrection. But Christ is alive, and the resurrected Christ can come into your heart and take the deadness of your soul and make it alive."

—Cathedral of the Resurrection, Moscow

"You have a soul, created in the image of God, and that soul is going to live forever—in heaven or hell. Our souls have been separated from God. What came between us and God? Sin! We have broken God's moral laws, and the Bible says we are all sinners. Our soul needs to be restored, and that is why Jesus Christ came. That's why He died on the cross. That's why He shed His blood and rose again, so that our souls could be restored and our sins can be forgiven, and we can have eternal life. What about your soul? Are you certain that your sins are forgiven? Do you know that if you died at this moment you would go to heaven? Don't play with your soul. Don't take a chance. Put your faith in Christ."

—Orthodox Cathedral, Novosibirsk

"The greatest need in the world is the transformation of human nature. We need a new heart that will not have lust and greed and hate in it. We need a heart filled with love and peace and joy, and that is why Jesus came into the world. He died on the cross to make peace between us and God, and to bring peace in our hearts. What do we have to do? There comes a time when we have to confirm for ourselves our own faith in Christ. It is not anything we can do to earn God's favor—it is only by faith and trust in Christ."

—Cathedral of the Epiphany, Moscow

The Media

"In every meeting, both public and private, I have spoken openly of my personal faith in the Lord Jesus Christ, and my conviction that Christ can solve the basic problem that causes so much turmoil in our lives and in our world—the problem of the human heart."

When Mr. Graham arrived in Moscow September 9, 1984 to begin his preaching tour, he was met by a strong force of the international press, representing major newspapers and magazines, television, and radio around the world.

Noting the intense schedule he had had during his 1982 visit, Mr. Graham said, "I did not talk enough to the press. But this time I was able to spend much more time with the press, and was able to answer their questions in more detail."

Many of the press stayed with Mr. Graham through his entire tour of the Soviet cities. Thus, the press chronicled Mr. Graham's visit to the world.

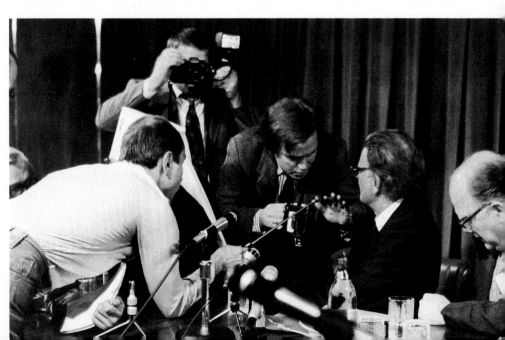

Of special interest was the coverage given by the Soviet media to Mr. Graham's visit. Normally the Soviet media does not report extensively on religious news, but in each city Mr. Graham's visit was chronicled by the local media. He also was interviewed frequently by Soviet reporters, and news of his trip was carried worldwide by Radio Moscow and the official Tass News Agency.

"I looked forward to having fellowship with my fellow Christians, and to meet a cross section of Soviet citizens. I also hoped to gain greater insight into Soviet society. Certainly these goals have been fulfilled."

Carl Mydens, one of America's most noted photojournalists who photographed Mr. Graham's tour for Time Magazine, was impressed with services throughout the tour. After Mr. Graham preached to a crowd of 3,000 jammed into the Leningrad Baptist Church, Mydens commented, "That was moving! That was tremendous! I have never seen anything like it." After photographing some of the services in the Russian Orthodox churches, Mydens said, "What a marvelous opportunity we have here, to be able to photograph these churches with all the television lights. No one may ever have this opportunity again!"

"Yes," said Billy Graham emphatically upon leaving the Soviet Union, "I definitely would classify this as one of the highlights of my ministry."

After all, he had preached to many thousands in four Soviet cities; he had spoken more than fifty times to church congregations, civic groups, and church and government leaders, including several members of the Central Committee of the Communist Party and a member of the Politburo. Of special interest were his discussions with Vladimir Kuroyedov, head of the Council for Religious Affairs, and his deputy, Vladimir Fitsev, who had played a major part in making the visit possible; Georgi Arbatov, director of the Institute of United States and Canadian Studies; Madam Meeta Vannas, the Vice-President of the Supreme Soviet of Estonia; and Yuri Zhukov, chairman of the Soviet Peace Committee and a former editor of *Pravda*. Most noteworthy, however, was his one-hour-and-forty minute meeting with Boris N. Ponomarev, Chairman of the International Relations Committee of the Central Committee of the Communist Party, and a member of the Politburo.

The schedule was the most intensive of Mr. Graham's forty-year ministry.

He had preached the Gospel, straightforward, unhindered, just as he has preached it all over the world. He had also covered a broad range of issues in his private discussion with political leaders, saying frankly that such issues as religious freedom and the imprisonment of unregistered believers are of real concern to American Christians and Jews and are serious barriers to closer relations with the Soviets. In private he had brought up the matters he considered to be of most serious concern:

from Dr. Andrei Sakharov (the well-known Soviet scientist and political dissident) and the oppression of Christians, to the almost complete lack of immigration of Jews. Mr. Graham visited synagogues in Moscow and Leningrad and talked candidly with rabbis and other Jewish leaders about their situation. In Moscow he conferred briefly with a delegation of independently registered Baptist pastors who are not members of the All-Union Council of Evangelical Christians-Baptists.

He listened with respect, he said, to those with whom he met, and tried to help them understand the concerns many persons in the United States and elsewhere in the world have about human rights and religious freedom.

A reporter asked if he had a feeling of success. "I think success is a relative term," Mr. Graham replied. "From God's point of view, I'll have to wait till I get to heaven and get the full report to see how successful we have been. From my point of view, wherever the Gospel is proclaimed, it's successful!"

He said all the goals he had set before going to the Soviet Union were fulfilled.

Apparently the Soviet people were aware that Billy Graham was in the Soviet Union and of what he was doing. His name is known there; nine of his books have been printed in the Russian language and are circulating there.

That his visit will have a lasting effect was noted in the fact that his message to the Russian Orthodox theological students at the academy in Leningrad was videotaped and will be used to help train Orthodox priests. Too, as Mr. Graham pointed out in a New York press conference after leaving the Soviet Union, "I think most church leaders were amazed at Soviet television, radio, and press coverage of our trip. One archbishop said he did not recall anything like it in his lifetime." The Soviet government had also permitted a western television crew to follow Mr. Graham's journey for a later prime time special on American and Canadian television; the crew received outstanding cooperation from the "Sovinfilm" organization.

He would not go so far as to say that a religious revival is afoot in the Soviet Union. "I did not have that much contact with the ordinary people," he said, "so I could not say that. There are people outside the Soviet Union who know the Soviet Union better than I do who say there is a religious interest on the part of Soviet citizens just as there is all over the world. It's a worldwide thing and I think part of it is due to the nuclear cloud that hangs over the world. People realize today that science is not going to save us and many people are turning to the metaphysical or they're turning to God or to a philosophy—it may be Buddhism, it may be Islam, it may be other religions—but they're turning to religion as something to believe in or to hold on to, just like some people turn to drugs or alcohol in times of difficulty.

"I also think one must say that the emphasis on peace that we heard so much of in the Soviet Union is a genuine thing," Mr. Graham said. "This goes for all the people of Europe—Eastern Europe as well as Western Europe—because they've had so many wars. One out of every twenty Soviet citizens was killed in World War II—twenty million fatalities. They can't get away from that because we're only a generation away from that war."

Noting that the Soviet Union's attitude toward the church sometimes changes with its foreign situation—toughening when its relations with the West become difficult—Mr. Graham said, "I don't know what might have been back of the Soviet government's plans, giving us such extensive entrees into meeting all these people. Yes, perhaps they were trying to use me, but in a sense I was using them to preach the Gospel and also to talk about peace. These terrible weapons we have created could destroy the world in a matter of hours, and we've got to have some dialogue with these people to live on the same planet. We've got to co-exist with them. I thought it would be good from both points of view to get a little better understanding. We trade with them. Why shouldn't a Gospel preacher talk with them? They never told me one time *what* to say or what I shouldn't—so I just stuck to the Gospel. There were restrictions on *where* I preached. I had to preach in the churches—on church property—not in any of the big stadiums." (By Soviet law religious meetings can only be held on church property).

Mr. Graham was satisfied that the 1984 trip confirmed the statements he made in 1982 for which he was criticized—the statement that he had found "a measure" of religious freedom in the Soviet Union.

"Many churches are open and active," he said, "and are allowed to carry out their work on church premises so long as they are registered as the law requires. At the same time, the Soviet Union does not allow churches to be a rallying point for what it considers to be anti-Soviet activities. Congregations that refuse to register run into difficulties and may face definite opposition from their government."

But in some areas, Mr. Graham found the Soviet people's manner of worship to be open and personal. "When I gave an invitation at the end of some services—not all, but some—for those in the audience to receive Jesus Christ, we would see anywhere from a dozen hands go up to the three hundred hands that my team counted in the Novosibirsk Baptist Church in Siberia. In that service at least half the audience was young people, and the church was packed tighter than any church I have ever seen."

Mr. Graham came away from the Soviet Union "with a better understanding of the Soviet people."

"I understand better the suffering and sacrifices they made during the Great Patriotic War," he said.

There was only one unfortunate incident on the tour. When Mr. Graham preached at the Moscow Baptist Church, the press was kept out of the church. The decision to bar the press was the church's decision alone; Mr. Graham was not aware of it in advance. A church official said the presence of the press turned the meeting into a show. "This was a service," he said, "not a show." Some press—both from the West and from the Soviet Union—reacted negatively to the restriction.

Among the memories that Mr. Graham will cherish are those of people standing with heads bowed, lips moving in prayer, of hundreds listening attentively to his every word—and of personal things: "Memories of a blind choir," he said, "in an Orthodox church; of little old ladies in black lighting candles in the churches; of a little girl eating soup in a kindergarten; of a little baby in Novosibirsk who opened his eyes and smiled—those are the personal memories I have."

Mr. Graham's final sermon in Moscow—and his last in the Soviet Union—was preached in the Cathedral of the Epiphany on "You Must Be Born Again." At the conclusion, Patriarch Pimen, head of the Russian Orthodox Church, said emphatically, "I think that God will help you . . . to visit our country again, and . . . deliver this same inspiring message."

Reflecting upon that statement later, Mr. Graham concluded, "If we are invited back, we will go, God willing, because I realize that God has given us a tremendous open door in Eastern Europe."

A Final Word By Billy Graham

Dear Reader,

My visit to four cities of the Soviet Union to preach the gospel of Jesus Christ was unquestionably one of the most memorable events of my entire ministry. I hope that through these pages you have sensed something of the excitement and opportunity of those days.

Only eternity will reveal the full results of that visit. However, in every church and in every city we saw countless people—young and old alike—respond to the Gospel and indicate their desire to follow Jesus Christ as Lord and Savior. In addition, many Christians have written me from the Soviet Union telling of the encouragement and the new vision for evangelism they received during those unforgettable days. Christians in the Soviet Union live in a society which is much different from ours, where religion is not encouraged and there is the constant pressure of atheistic propaganda. And yet God is at work, and the dedication and joy of the Christians we met is a challenge and an inspiration.

I came away from the Soviet Union convinced more than ever that Christ—and only Christ—can meet the deepest needs of our world and our hearts. Christ alone can bring lasting peace—peace with God, peace among men and nations, and peace within our hearts.

He transcends the political and social boundaries of our world, for beneath the surface people everywhere are basically the same. The deeper, spiritual needs of the human heart are universal—the hunger for God, the need for forgiveness, the yearning for hope and eternal life. And Christ can meet those needs, for He came into this world to give us salvation and restore us to God.

I will never forget one man we met from Leningrad. He told about living in the midst of the horror and suffering of the 900 Day Siege of Leningrad during World War Two. Fighting swirled around him, starvation and disease ravaged the population, and he knew every minute could be his last. But, he told us, in the midst of the terror and uncertainty of war he found true peace in his heart, because he found Christ. I will never forget the joy on his face.

Just as Christ touched that man, so Christ can touch your life and give you the peace you are seeking. Just as we saw hundreds do in the Soviet Union, so you can open your heart right now to Jesus Christ and ask Him to forgive you and save you. Don't let another day go by without making your commitment to Christ.

Billy Graham